A Book of Poetry

Volume I

JACKIE-JOE B JACKSON

Published by Victorious You Press™
Charlotte NC, USA

TITLE: A BOOK OF POETRY
First Printed: 2023

Cover Designer: NADIA MONSANO
Editor: SHAYANA OAKLEY

ISBN: 978-1-952756-93-1
ISBN: (eBook) 978-1-952756-94-8
Library of Congress Control Number: 2023900335

Printed in the United States of America

For details email joan@victoriousyoupress.com
or visit us at www.victoriousyoupress.com

Dedication

This book is dedicated to my mother Everil Codling and my father James Jackson.

Acknowledgements

Thanks to my mother, Everil Codling, who is always there for me and continually cheers me on.

I want to thank my family for their love, encouragement and support. Thanks to Julian Walker, my lifelong friend, who always had confidence in my writing. You persistently nudged me over the years to continue writing my poetry and to publish my words for others to read.

Table of Content

A Tribute for Kenny

He was one of us
Life… so precious, yet unjust
Today he is no more
My heart aches I feel sore
Let's not mourn for Kenny
Instead let's celebrate him
He was a med student
Only twenty-one
He was someone's son
Destined for all that we seek
Yet he left us feeling bleak
Let's keep him with us
In our thoughts
In our studies
In our goals
Let's do this thing, not only for ourselves
But for Kenny
Whether you are a past student
Present
Or have a far way to go
Let's keep Kenny alive
Remember his family
His loved ones
His friends
Let his circumstance motivate us
To carry the torch & continue this journey

Medicine was Kenny's dream
We will carry his dream with us
Today and forever
He was a Med one student
So are we
Now let's see
Together we fight
With all our might
Let's get this done
For Kenny, someone's son

Jackie-Joe

Introduction

I have always enjoyed reading and writing poetry. I started writing poems at the age of 15. It started with short rhymes while attending school in Jamaica, where I was born. Over the years, poetry became my favorite hobby and best way of expressing my thoughts. In my twenties, three of my poems were published and can be found once googling my maiden name, Jackie-Joe Jackson. Writing poetry makes me feel happy and fulfilled. So much happens on a daily basis and poetry is my way of capturing and expressing my experiences.

Poetry began as a hobby, until I truly experienced life. Falling in love, having a family, establishing a relationship with God, things I have witnessed, politics, social life, the economy and so much more, gave me the drive to continuing writing. Poetry gives me joy and pleasure, especially seeing others' reactions when reading it. The glow and enthusiasm screams, " I want more, I want more!" This first volume of poetry is the beginning of documenting my life experiences and speaking on current events. I hope to share my poems with the world and that my audience/readers enjoy reading them. Thank you for your support and love of poetry.

Everyday Life Events

SECTION I

Who Is That Individual?

She/He is whoever she/he identify
Why do we need to classify
Ze/Per/Hir/They is a daughter
Ze/Per/Hir/They is a son
Ze/Per/Hir/They is a child
Ze/Per/Hir They is a friend
Who doesn't pretend
She/He is a mother
Sometimes even a father
This Girl/Boy is bold
At least that's what she/he has been told
This boy is shy
People wonder why he doesn't stay as a guy
They say he is confused
But he refuses
He chooses
Once born a different gender
Society tries to hinder
She/He identifies as they
She/He identifies as a girl
She /He is a woman
She/He is a man
Ze/Per/Hir/They
Gender neutral as it may
She/her
They/Them
He/him
Expresses truly who lies within

What's Your Talent?

My T Is for Talented
My A Is for Aspiration
My L is for Longevity
My E is for Empowerment
My N Is for Nurturing
My T is for Teachable

What's yours?

You Were Once My Friend

She was a best friend
How did this end?
Don't know where to start
I've often wondered…how did we part?
Was it jealousy
Of my legacy
My intellectual property
Or my personality?
We once did everything together
My innermost self-thought this would last forever
Was it me?
Can't be…
We were so near
But yet so far
I often think of you
I wonder do you think of me too?
Some friends come and go
As you well know
I wish you all the best
But now I lay this friendship to rest

That Tattoo

That Tattoo…
You know the one
It's different
You designed it to be effervescent
But…really
Your upper inner thigh
Why, why, why?
An ice cream cone with dripping pistachio
Might as well say Jackie-O
To top it off
You wrote below
Eat me
Wild choice
Wouldn't you agree?

These Walls Have Ears

These Walls Have Ears
Shhh, listen
Did you hear those tippy toes?
Wait…is that the crackling sound on the wooden floor?
Speak quietly
These walls have ears
Ears that do not hear clearly
Did you hear what was repeated?
Wow, so farfetched I can't conceal it
First, it's the shock that you tried to eavesdrop
Ear hustle…I said I dreaded it
You said you heard…I bedded him
Shhh, listen
Speak quietly
These walls have ears
Thought I'd share

Secrets

I have a secret…or a few
Do you?
Ummm…
Secrets are meant to be unseen
From other human beings
Some secrets are untold
Unknown by other souls
Some secrets are a mystery
Maintaining it… quietly
Despite…peering inquiries
Today I will reveal one of my most sacred secrets
Known only by a few friends and family
Are you ready?
This secret…is
One of my favorite hobbies
Have you guessed it yet?
Now that we've met
I…wait…
Tis a bait
I secretly write poetry
Finally revealed to those in this society

Remember When?

Remember when your bank was a little piggy?
Felt nice when you shook it...and it was jiggy
Now we have banks galore
Everyday opened to explore
Did you know of Apple Pay
Money received same day?
Do you remember when a beeper
Was your communication to him/her?
Then came the flip phone
Computers...dial up
Floppy disc
iCloud
Wireless?
Nevertheless
Now we have Bluetooth
Music connected...coming through
Wi-Fi
Umm, I must sigh
Do you remember the recent gossips about the insurrection?
Or Bible stories of Jesus's resurrection?
Wait a minute, bell foot pants
Once extinct...now everyone wants
Remember when you were a boyfriend/girlfriend?
Fiancée...
Watch out for the finances
Prenup...

Sign here? Yup!
Now you're a wife or a husband
Remember when you made plans?
How to become someone
The evolution of time
Is simply divine

The One Who Got Away

Have you ever wondered
How did I get here?
Why is this happening?
The one who got away
Why didn't he stay?
Was it her?
Let's infer
Let's consider time
Or were we no longer aligned?
Did we grow apart?
This breaks my heart
Move on you say
In the moment, I feel dismayed
I have loved you for more than half my life
I tried extremely hard to be a dutiful wife
But instead, I became the enabler
Now I feel like a stranger
How did you mess up this big?
Surely, you did not think
Such behavior would not sink
Us
Thus
The one who got away
Is now on her merry way

Why Do I Shop?

I asked him for a title
He felt entitled
So, he nonchalantly spat out
These surprising words from his mouth
Why do you shop?
Wow, I thought
After all I just said
All my poems I've just read
As my brain spirals
Hitting the keys on my MacBook Air
Does he truly care?
Why do I shop?
Is that all you've got?
I shop because I can
In spite of anyone
Questioning my desires
Why do I shop?
I enjoy nice things
I shop to fulfill my needs
I shop because it makes me happy
Yet my shopping makes him upset
My mood is offset
This title he gave me
Jolted my psyche
Why do I shop?
I shop because I can

Nurse Practitioners

Nurse Practitioners
Are nurturers
They are trustworthy
Never in a hurry
They assess, diagnose & treat
Oh, what a relief
Always a nurse first
Lifelong learning always a thirst
Advocating for others
One of the NP's greatest mantras
Competent, dedicated & smart
Works independently, their own business now started
Look how far we've come
From Florence Nightingale
Her teachings we embrace
Known as "The Lady with the Lamp"
Hey Nurse B, give that IV, remember to use that clamp
Accuracy, thoroughness
Blended with thoughtfulness
Kind and ethical
Nurse Practitioners are practical
Always a nurse first
Distinctive qualities...thus emerge
Detailed oriented
Always authentic
Awesome listeners

Givers, not takers
Movers and shakers
Essential workers
Patients love us
Innovative and strategic
Nurses…Nurse Practitioners
Some now have full practice authority
I love this profession
The emblem of my succession

The Power Of Words

Some words are spoken simple
Others are complicated
But whenever we speak
Remember who is our audience
As we seek to understand
The meaning of the message
Even at times when we speak with such passion and zealous
People please do not be jealous
Speaker- take care to deliver your words
Listener- take heed, listen keenly
Ask for explanation
During your discussion
Some words taste sweet on the lips
Some are spoken more often
As they become our favorites
Words by themselves are just words
But putting the right words together can be very powerful
Very meaningful
Choose your words carefully
As you articulate your verbiage
Be mindful of your audience

Spiritual

SECTION II

My Journey To Righteousness

God is love and I am blessed
I give thanks everyday even during this mess
This pandemic crisis
Government's indecisive
War and rumors of war
As we are here on earth shooting for the star
The end is near my brothers and sisters
Please register and recognize this
I'm on my journey to discover my own righteousness
Seeking to find my salvation
Yearning for peace
Looking to increase
My wisdom, understanding and purpose
Sometimes I'm quite nervous
But I'm fully committed to press on
My faith in God is all I have
I am not rich with money
But I'm enriched by his blessings, holiness, and examples
He said, ask...and though shall receive
Seek and he shall find
My journey to discover my righteousness continues
As I attempt to walk in Jesus' shoes
Those are almighty shoes to fit
But I will continue to commit
I surrender my heart and my soul to you dear Lord

As I continue working my way to you
My journey to discover my righteousness continues

God Of My Salvation

God of my salvation

Please help those in starvation
Thank you for your greatness
Thank you for all your mercies
You are a blessing
To all of your children
I pray for us to be risen
To seek you first
Dear Lord I thirst
For my salvation
Thank you for your mercies
God I am a Christian by heart
Life on Earth is really hard
Challenges, test of faith
But oh, mighty Lord you are so great
I remain thankful
Lord you are so graceful
Thank you for all your greatness
Your forever blessings
I pray for your forgiveness
I pray that I can be as humble
As a lamb
Innocent as a child
Steadfast in your glory
God you are so holy

I love you above all other
Thank you, Lord, for giving me life
You are almighty and strong
Showing us mercy even when we feel we do not belong
Thus…
Without you, life does not matter
Dear Lord I pray for your mercy upon us
Thus…
I long to live in heaven by your side
I will continue to abide
Living by your words
Doing your work
To God be the glory
Dear God, you are the greatest part of my story

The Prayer Line

The prayer line
Simply divine
Brothers and sisters gathered in faith
I cannot wait
For each day
Every gathering
All of us praying
Some of us openly
Some of us silently
We give testimonials
Each so influential
On our beliefs
Empowering our faith
Whilst we wait
For our salvation
We continue to give devotion
Singing his praise
Discussing God's ways
His guidance
For this audience
Empowering each other
Supporting one another
Putting God first
For our salvation we thirst
Thankful for his son Jesus
He is always with us
The prayer line
Simply divine

The Lord Thy Savior

The Lord thy Savior
Peace in this dark world of sin
I pray we let the Lord in
No weapon forms against you
Will ever come through
The devil will continue to tempt us
Do not waste your time to let him inside
Satan get behind us
We are the children of God
Seek God's words as well described
Your life as it's prescribed
No more panic
God is the King of peace
Let your heart just trust in his word
When you trust in God
He will always lead you
Open your brain
The knowledge of God
As revealed in Christ
We must have Jesus
He will protect us
Thus
Jesus died for our sins
To guide us
To protect us
To teach us

To keep us
To love us
To give us life
To give us hope and strengthen our relationship with God
The trinity
God lives within

God Is Love

God is love
All the time
His power, is truly divine
His love is unconditional
Truly inspirational
Just lift up your eyes
Open your heart and receive his love
He is our protector
And our Savior
He is mighty
He loves us so much that he gave his only son
Jesus
To show us... how to truly live
God wants us to love as he does
Forgive others
Even when they have wronged us
God is our light and our salvation
God is amazing
There is no other
So, my sisters and brothers
Continue to believe in him
He said ask and thou shall receive
Seek and he shall find
Speak love into your heart
Love one another
As God has loved us

Keep on praying
In silence, in groups, in Church, in your home
He hears and answers our prayers
God is an on time God
And he is our Savior

Political

SECTION III

A Wah Dis (patois)

A Wah Dis?
Lawd…Miss
Disya catastrophe
Inna disya pandemic
Dem buy out the toilet paper
Nuffi mention the sanitizer
Masks? Wat?
Don't even chat bout dat
De people dem gaan wile
But whole heep a COVID child
Born inna disya time
Me glad none a mine
De poor ting dem caan even see face
Half a di face dem cover up
Disya pandemic really rough
People start feel down
Like dem inna the ground
Everyone a wanda
How much longa
Pockets a bun
Watch fe de gun
Dem a loot and shoot
Babylon a gwaan bad
Me caan breed hima cry
Me neck unda dem knees
Now him lef ded

People a act like dem mad
Help! Dem say
Wat a dismay
Dis affi change
Government mus rearrange
Look pan disya pandemic
It epic!
Look how much life you take
You see all de people you break
Hurry up and gwaan Covid
You damn big head morbid

What Is This? (English version)

What is this?
Lord...Miss
This catastrophe
In this pandemic
People bought all the toilet paper
Not to mention all the sanitizer
Masks? What?
Don't even speak about that
These people are going wild
There's a lot of COVID child
Born during this time
I'm glad that none are mine
These poor babies can't see your face
Half of our face is covered up
This pandemic is rough
People are feeling down
As if they are in the ground
Everyone is wondering
How much longer?
Pockets are burning
Look out for that gun
People are looting and shooting
Police are going bad
I can't breathe
He cries
While under the knees

He is now dead
Individuals are acting as if they are mad
HELP! They say
This is such a dismay
Things must change
Our government needs to rearrange
Look at this pandemic
Its epic!
Look how many lives you've taken
Look at all those lives you have broken
Hurry up and leave COVID
You are a damn big head morbid

The Insurrection

Is this our America
¿Me hermosa país?
Miércoles 6 de enero de 21
What is really going on?
This all-day marathon
It was the middle of the week
Most did not see
The uproar
The wrath of the sword
Raging through the Capitol
They need to be calm with some propranolol
Is this my USA?
The country they say
Venez tous
Democracy
Or autocracy?
My oh my
I continuously sigh
SMH
These disruptive individuals
Pseudo or non-intellectuals?
How does one even justify?
They will all have to testify
For all that they've done
Bang! Bang!
They just killed someone

Is this for real?
This terrorist attack
Lawd me caan relate to dat
An attack on our democracy
Yet there are some with hypocrisy
Snarling...this is not an attack
It is a demonstration
A weh yu come from man?
Oh, what a tragedy
Such a dismay
Yet they say
The election was rigged
The head one reneged
I pray for some semblance of normalcy
In this America the land of my democracy

Breaking News

Fourteen children killed
Where? In Texas
When? 5/24/22
Again?
Killed? Are you sure they are dead?
Yes, it's breaking news
Not a fuse
Anyone else
Yes...one teacher
Four more children
And one teenager
That said teenager was the suspect
All died
This act is vile
Nineteen...young lives
Murdered...gunned down
This violence
Occurred at an elementary school
What a ruse
So many lives lost
At what cost?
Who is to be blamed?
This is utterly insane
Wait, the count is now eighteen
What a massacre
So many lives to mourn

How is this possible?
Why does this keep happening
Here in the USA?
What a dismay
Catastrophic
So many lives affected
My heart truly hurts
I feel unearthed
Numb even
I'm wondering, when will this violence end?
Who is responsible
For this inhumane act of liberty?
Such destructivity
Screaming for help
Saying, "Please stop this hateful shooting!"
Find some other useful activity
How can we help those who are lost?
How will they pay and at what cost?
Lord, have mercy upon those children who witnessed this
devastating
Traumatic event
Give strength and hope to all those affected by this sad situa-
tion
That occurred in our nation
Breaking News
Horrific and yet such different views

Social Media

Social media
So influential
Gives us pleasure
Enjoying at leisure
No matter how simple
Or grand
Those pictures
Surely tells us stories
Some more meaningful
Some...truly hateful
Social media
Have all the words from old school encyclopedia
Google rhymes with doodle
Meets my approval
As a search engine
I can find most things within
Facebook, Instagram, WhatsApp
All have now merged
Twitter
Tik Tok
All have lots of followers
Ideas mimicked...even some borrowers
Social media
Allows you to truly express
Whatever your heart desires

Nature

SECTION IV

My Hummingbird

The hummingbird is my spirit animal
Remains national
The Trochilus Polytmus
Called the "Doctor Bird"
Also known as "Swallowtail"
He is a hummingbird
Have you heard?
The hummingbird is sacred
With special qualities
He is spiritual
Symbolizes healing
Represents joy
Represents good luck
He is peace
He is colorful
He is graceful
He is beautiful
He is one of a kind
Truly divine
He is indigenous
From the land of my birth
Upon this Earth
I wear him as a tattoo
I chose him for my logo
This is his photo
My beautiful hummingbird

The Rise Of Dawn

I woke up early this morning
I feel alive
I saw the beautiful, golden sunlight
I feel the cool air across my face as it tickles the hair along
my earlobe
I feel alive
I feel an indescribable energy
A wave of life unfolds
I feel alive
I inhale
I slowly exhale
I smile as I took the first sip of my morning coffee
I feel alive
I hear the chirping of a bird
I hear the barking of a dog
I hear silence
I feel alive
My heart feels good
My brain is clear
I feel alive
I am fulfilled
Enjoying nature at her fullest
I wake up at dawn
I am alive!

The Characters Of Trees

This tree stands tall
This tree is short
Her leaves spread so wide
Providing shade
Protecting me from the blazing sun
Now comes the thunderstorm
Where's this coming from?
She starts to sway
Now…today
She stands very still
Her beautiful leaves now scant
As if she went on a rampage
Then I look up again
She is now bent at the waist
I look on the ground
The tree roots are still standing strong
This tree went through a lot
But still, she remains in her spot

Zi Zy Zen

Zi Zy Zen
Shhh, be quiet
I'm trying as hard as I might
To find my center
Please do not enter
Zi Zy Zen
Please don't end
My brain needs to rest
Not hear all about your fuss
Shhh, by quiet
You sound as if there's a riot
Zi Zy Zen
Will this ever end?
I just need a little time alone
In my zen zone
Shhh, be quiet
You just might
Find some peace of mind
Just be a little kind
Zi Zy Zen
This is my daily Amen

Pink & Purple

I love the color purple
A color you will always find in my inner circle
Pink was once my favorite color
Especially when seen on flowers
As I grew older
My love for pink grew stronger
Pink represents harmony
She looks great against ivory
The epitome of my soul
Whenever I wear pink, I feel like I am in control
Pink represents inner peace
Oh, what a release
She also stands for friendship and affection
Did I forget to mention?
Pink represents approachability...that's truly me
My favorite once pink now embraced with purple
Purple represents parts of my true identity
That of creativity and dignity
Purple stands for nobility
She is the color of royalty
Purple represents pride and independence
Symbolic to my very existence
I love the color purple
Because she stands out like magic
Whenever I wear her, she makes me feel enigmatic

Love

SECTION V

Forever My Valentine

To the love of my life

I love you

I adore you

I admire you

I care for you

Words cannot express

So, I must confess

How much with each day that passes by

I look to the sky

My heart grows fonder

My love grows stronger

My life is better with you in it

I will never quit

On us...

Thus...

I have loved you from the first day we met

I have no regret

You are my one true love

Sent from above

Withstanding the end of time

Forever my Valentine

The Forever Letter

To whom it may concern:

Dear my forever

This is a letter of declaration
I am writing you this letter
To inform you that effective immediately
I declare my love for you
I wish you peace and tranquility
Love and unity
I ask that you have a fulfilled life
One that's meaningful
Enjoy each day as if it could be your last on this Earth
Take a breath
Inhale, then exhale
Remember to always put God first
In all that you do
Pray before you go to bed
Pray as you first open your eyes
Give thanks and praise that he woke you up this morning
Ask God for forgiveness
Seek your own righteousness
Surrender your heart to God
Now more than ever the words of Revelation have come to
pass
I love you and I will continue to pray for you

You are the light of my life
Please know that I will always love you
My dearest friend forever

Love Is Powerful

Love is powerful
Love is kind
Love is pure
Love is true
Love does not hurt
Love is giving
Love is patient
Love is not envious
Love is transparent
Love is humble
Love is gracious
All these are true about love
Unless environmental changes occur
Love can change quickly to hate
Let love conquer all
Do not fall
Stand strong embrace love
In its entirety
Love is wonderful, amazing
Love is powerful

Forgiveness

Forgiveness is very hard to do
Especially when someone has done wrong by you
But it is so important that we learn how to
Ask for forgiveness
And to forgive others
When we ask for forgiveness
We feel better once we receive it
Forgiveness starts with God
But when we love and hurt others
And they forgive us
We just
Feel happy and light in our hearts
We feel loved
When we forgive others
We feel relieved in our hearts
We feel light and unburdened
Forgiveness allows us to be able to let go
Even feel loved
Forgiveness feels like a dove

Life As We Know It

Life as we know it
People get a grip
Life is too short
Time waits for no man
Follow your dreams
No matter what or how hard it may seem
Redeem yourself
Tomorrow is not promised to us
So maybe just
Follow your heart
Even if you feel your dream seems too far
Fetched
Just edged into today
Life as you know it
May change in the blink of an eye
Love and live your life
As you know it
Keep that wit

Hope

SECTION VI

The Child Left Behind

My sweet child, I wonder what's on your mind?
A sense of loneliness
She feels loss
She feels sad
She is disappointed
But she's determined
Despite all odds
She plugs through this earth
Forever, seeking something
Unsure of herself
But she's determined
To find her way
To discover love
Seeking more
More of what?
Just more, more, more
She can't fill that void inside of her
Separation from family
She feels judged
She feels alone
She feels like an on outcast
The prodigal child
Why was she left behind?
She continues to persevere
Through hope and faith

She looks to God
She prays for wisdom, love and happiness
God answers her prayers
Despite all the naysayers
The child left behind
Her smile is divine
She grew up
She found her wisdom, love, and happiness
But she's determined
She now searches for righteousness
She is blessed and she knows now that she was never left behind
She discovered something
God was with her through every moment in time, even when she had doubt
She knows now there's no child left behind

The Invitation

What's an invitation?
It can be verbal or written
What is the purpose?
Shhh…he's about to propose
It's a wedding invitation
Such an auspicious occasion
This invite is so delicately wrapped
But I feel a little trapped
First let's look at the date
Where, when and what time?
Time for people to shine
I can't wait to taste the cake
I feel so happy for the couple
Once single, now double
I imagine her beautiful dress
With the groom at his utmost best
Wait…it's another invitation
This venue is at a fire station
I have been sanctioned
Hey, cheer up, it's a party!
Let's have fun and be hearty
The best invitation
Is yet to come
It's a very special one
This is an invitation to my heart
Hey! Let's start

Knock and I will let you in
Here's a glance of who lies within
Her love for you is so precious
This invitation is infamous
With a huge incentive
It's not expensive
The invitation is delicate
So precious, there's no duplicate
Such joy and delight
Accept my invitation because it feels right

The Forgotten One

The forgotten one
How does this happen?
Where did you go?
Time…then, now, the future
Have you no one?
Once thought you were special
Had so many "friends"
Or so you thought
Now you're wrought
Forgotten
But all of a sudden
Left all alone
Lost in the zone
Will someone find you? I wonder
As you sit and ponder
Once well-known
Now feeling all alone
The forgotten one
No more…I'm sure
Once forgotten
Misbegotten
Although so common
Now you recall
They thought you'd fall
All will remember
Born...the 10th of November

A Rollin' Stone

You are a rollin' stone
She says
You will gather no moss
Now I am boss
How can you say those words
To a young, growing girl?
Seeking to find her way
Upon this Earth
Yet you spat dirt
Words that truly hurt
But hurt as they may
This girl remained
Focused
Just…
Determined to make her roots
Finding her true purpose
A rollin' stone
Stay tuned
She is just getting started
Empower...persevere…achieve
This girl continues to believe
One day she will find her peace

What Are Your Needs?

Some need love and affection
Not to mention
Others need food and water
Oh yes, listen my daughter
Shelter, even better
We all need money
But how much
Is enough to cover your bills?
Or do you need more for the unforeseen?
Some yearn for simplicity
But it's difficult in the society
As commercials
Social media
Often times influence
What others think, that's what I need
Salvation
Everlasting life
Brothers and sisters when we place God first
We will never thirst
We will never be in need
Our God is strong, powerful and mighty
He loves us, he forgives us
Place God first
Have faith
Believe in him
All will be possible

Dreams

SECTION VII

Hidden Gem

She's such a beauty
But she doesn't know it
A hidden gem
Everyone knows this
She smiles and your heart melts
She's such a beauty
But she doesn't know it
She walks with grace
She speaks eloquently
She's loved by everyone
She's young but so bold
She's such a beauty
But she doesn't know it
Even when she cries
She's such a beauty
She cares about everyone and everything
She loves her dog
Her baby girl
She's such a beauty
But she doesn't know it
A hidden gem
So rare and precious
Her heart so pure and kind
She gives of herself completely
In spite of the hurt that lies within

She pours her heart out
As she bleeds on the inside
She still gives all of herself
She's such a beauty
A hidden gem
Every life, she does touch
People respect her so much
She's imperfectly perfect
This girl has all my respect
She's such a beauty
A hidden gem
Loved by all of them
She has so much zest
She deserves the best

Some I Admire

Some are famous people
But not all are celebrities
It could be our friends or families
I admire people for certain qualities
Some more than others
One of my favorites is my mother
But I can't stop there
I would not dare
Because I love Miss Louis Bennett
My first introduction to poetry
"Nutin fi naam "
Do you remember that one?
I was a little girl
Dressed in my mother's pearl
A bit stage fright
But I stood there ready to fight
I performed that skit
It was quite legit
In recital mode
Posed and dressed to code
I received lots of cheers
I wish you were there
To bear witness to this
It was truly amidst
Afterwards I started writing my own poems

As a hobby at first
But the more I wrote the more I thirst
Maya Angelou…
She was definitely another of my idols
"And Still I Rise"
Words truly strong and wise
Young, upcoming poet
Amanda Gorman
"The Hill We Climb"
This poem so precious and divine
I admire and love Oprah
I also admire and love Ellen D
You know who I mean
Both women truly iconic
Sade…
Dare I say
She's my favorite singer
A middle name I gave my daughter
Denzel, Will Smith
Julia Roberts
Old school but they will always be famous
Halle B
Cardi B
Jada and Queen Latifah
Have you seen the Equalizer?
Shonda…you are such a wonder
You are such an inspiration
Megan…thee Stallion…

All above-mentioned is a reiteration
There are so many others
For those of us
Ready...to...bussss
All of your work is so diverse
You are all so special in this universe

Intermission

This is an intermission
Wait, what's next?
I wonder what's the surprise?
Is it worthwhile?
Am I just a bit eager
To know what's coming up?
Is it a continuum
Or a new part?
Restart
This intermission has me on edge
Change is scary, sometimes
Yet necessary
As the saga continues
Let's see what the end brings
I hope its fulfilling

The Closing of This Chapter

This journey has been long
It has been challenging
But it has also been perfect
With every trial and tribulation
We move through life
In stages, always moving through
Although we may have specific dreams
Our lives are already spoken for
It is part of the heavenly design
As for mine
I am a dreamer
I am a planner
I am a doer
I am a believer
When I dream of doing anything
I start by praying
I send up all my prayers to God
God listens and he answers my prayers
I trust him
I fear him
But I honor and I worship him
When I walk, drive, am at home, at church, in any given moment
I magnify his name
I am rich in his spirit
And I am blessed in his name

We may think where we are today is the end
But if you have hopes, dreams and other aspirations
Ask God, if it is for you and it will happen
God is an on-time God
He is mighty and just
Just trust
In God and be patient
Keep on dreaming
Keep on praying
This life is forever changing
As we move forward
Embrace each day as if it is your last
The closing of this chapter
Does not mean the end
It is just the beginning of a new one

Inspirational

SECTION VIII

What's Your True Worth?

Some may think of true worth in millions
Others may even think billions
But my true worth…
Truth, unearth
I believe in myself
This in and of itself
Has ignite my passion
For having compassion
For love of fashion
Whether in scrubs or dressed like the Kardashians
For caring of others
Just like my mother
Love of family
Value of integrity
Hard work and dedication
Love of self
Love of others
The gift of sharing
The wonderful feeling of caring
Understanding sadness
Even in times of madness
Rising amongst all odds
Recognizing those subtle nods
Defying those who attempt to keep me down
Always smiling, never a frown
Treating others with dignity

Brutal as it may but always honesty
I will never subdue
I will always pursue
Value of self and others…this is my true worth

Hello Beautiful

Hello beautiful she says
As she greets you with each passing day
Enlightens your heart
Makes one feel as if a fresh start
Hi beautiful
Makes you feel wonderful
I feel like I'm embracing the world
As my head swirled
Hello beautiful she says
Even with her past tribulations and trials
She maintains a positive attitude that one admires
Hi beautiful
You make life meaningful
May God continue to bless you
For all the amazing things that you do
Hello beautiful
Your presence so effervescent and plentiful

Life Changing Decisions

You have one life to live
So, live it
You have choices to make
Choose wisely
Do not make decisions in a hurry
But do not tarry
Recognize when it is time to make changes
As difficult as those may be
Know your worth
Acknowledge your likes and dislikes
Value and love yourself
Open your eyes to nonsense
Use commonsense
Remember others and your experience
Do not lose yourself in the midst of this life
Find out who you are
Stand for something
If not, you will be left with nothing
It is never too late
To date
If that is what worries you
Do not worry about tomorrow
Let tomorrow worry about itself
Be happy with who you are
Reach for your star
Do not let others live for you

You MUST choose
We all have the freedom of choice
Use your voice
Watch for actions
Do you have total satisfaction?
Are you fulfilled?
Or just going through the motion of living
Life changing decisions
Must be part of your self-actualization

Frustration (patois)

Lawd wat a piece a frustration
Dis a one bad situation
Everyway me look
Me dis a get block
Me pray
Me swear
Me give up
Den me haffi seh cho mek me git up
Wah kinda sense dis mek
Me fi dis lay down and tek
Nah sah dis naa gudung so
Frustration gwaan bout
Ca me ready fi dashout
You caan keep me down
Me bout fi smile and leggo disya frown
Fi me faith too strong
Gwaan bout yu business satan
And mek sure you carry out frustration

Frustration (English version)

Lord this is such a frustration
This is a bad situation
Everywhere I look
I keep getting blocked
I pray
I swear
I give up
Then I have to decide to get up
This makes no sense
I cannot just lay down and take this
Not at all, this will not go on like this
This frustration needs to go away
Because I am ready to move on
I will not let my situation keep me down
I will continue to smile, no more frowning
My faith is too strong
Satan, go away
And take this frustration with you

Divine Intervention

Divine Intervention
As I walked away in anger
Disappointment
Bothered about my situation
I went to a quiet place
In my own space
I intended to make plans
But I started talking to my friends
Wow! Lots of opinions
But still no resolution
I got a hot stone massage
Had a nice conversation
With my massage therapist
But still, at the end
Reality hit
I felt alone
So, I went into a zone
As I prayed for guidance
Seeking directions
I was given the answer
In the midst of my dismay
God sent his angel
And I started an online search
I decided to apply to med school
And lo and behold I got through
I do not know how

But through my trials and tribulations
There was truly divine intervention
God sent his angel
To lead me to my longtime dream
As difficult as it may seem
I have a lot on my plate
But I know that God will always prevail
There is nothing God cannot do
And I believe in him and I know he will carry me through

Family

SECTION IX

For My Mother

Mom, I love you endlessly
You have been my greatest inspiration
With your deep, kind devotion
Loving me unconditionally
My dearest mother
There is no other
Who will understand me
Let me just be
I am always reaching for the stars
Without any reservations
Just pure perseverance
You are my first love
You were sent from above
To be my mother
Allowing me to be a part of this Earth
You gave me birth
I am so thankful to you
For everything that you do
Even when we disagree
I still see
The meaning of your words
Have truly been heard
You are my first love
Your heart's as pure as a dove

The Half Siblings

The half sibling
Is truly a thing
In my family
Let's check in
Born the eighth of eight
From my mom
I believe the second of eight
From my dad
Sixteen! I've counted
Truly dumbfounded
All seven from mom share the same father
Except for me
And only the twins from my father
Share the same mother
I grew up, for the most part,
With my siblings from my mother
Always trying to be close
To the siblings I know the most
But I often wonder
Most times I sit and ponder
How can I reach out
To siblings who are strangers
I've contemplated engaging
Maybe getting to know them all
If even in a small way
A reunion?

Let's start with some communication
I've decided to make an effort
For what it's worth
To rekindle
With all of my half siblings

Family

Family consists of parents
Children and descendants
Here is the word 'family' simplified
F is for Father
A is for Ancestors
M is for Mother
I is for Infinite
L is for Love
Y is for yours

I Am

I am a mother
I am a child
They say that I am the glue that holds my family
But I am
Just me
Truly trying to fulfill my duties and my life on this Earth
From the day of my birth
I was born prematurely
But surely
I am still here
I cannot bear
Thoughts of not helping
My family, a friend or a stranger
Even if it's just pure words or kindness
I am
A true believer in the strength of family
The unity of family
I am the planner
The peace maker
The caregiver
I am a woman
Who stands by anyone
Whether or not he/she is a challenge
I am able to manage
To stay focused
And just
Be a member of my family

Too Late

Too late they say
Now that I am gone through the gate
Little to no appreciation
From thy family
Family can make
Or break you
Tis' your decision to stay
Be enslaved
Or seek your peace
Love your family from afar
Somewhere under the star
Too late
You did not know who I was
When you continued to make a fuss
Thus
All I seek is to fit in
No matter how much work I have had to put in
Relationships in a family is important
For everyone
Even as the glue
Often becomes loose
Now I have had enough
I will always love you
But I can no longer love you from here
No, not so near
But I can love you from afar

I can no longer stay
Things have gone too far
And now it is too late

For My Dad

I love my dad
His spirit is in me
He helped shape the woman I have become
And I will forever be thankful
He loves to dance
And so do I
My children as well
My dad's genetics are very strong
He always encouraged me along
Dad, I remember you
And all that you do
Even though we are oceans apart
You remain in my heart
I love you dad
I feel so sad
That we are so far from each other
But always know you have the love of this daughter

ABOUT THE AUTHOR

Jackie-Joe Jackson holds a Doctor of Nursing Practice Degree (DNP) & is a Family Nurse Practitioner. In addition, she is an Adjunct Professor for Widener University Mentor & Preceptor for Family Nurse Practitioners.

Jackie-Joe is a dynamic, results-driven, established DNP. She has solid business acumen, a Master of Science in Nursing (MSN), and 15+ years of hands-on experience in patient-centric roles. She is an expert at working collaboratively with a high-performing team of healthcare professionals, driving optimum levels of patient care, treatment, and results. In addition, she is dedicated to furthering personal and professional development through ongoing education and training initiatives and adherence to nursing best practices.

She loves dancing, reading, writing poetry & other books. She also enjoys spending quality time with my family, traveling & having coffee in the morning with her first love, her mother, Everil Codling.

Jackie-Joe is the mother of two adult children, Dante White & Samantha- Joe Lindo and her dog JoJo Chanel.